This Christmas Coloring Book
Belongs To:

____

____

Write and Draw to Express Yourself

Date: _____ / ___ / ___

Date: _______ / ___ / _______

Write and Draw to Express Yourself

Date: ___/___/___

Date: _______ / ___ / ___

Write and Draw to Express Yourself

Write and Draw to Express Yourself

Date:

Write and Draw to Express Yourself

Date: ____ / ____ / ____

Date: _____/_____/_____

Write and Draw to Express Yourself

Date: ___ / ___ / ___

Date: _____/____/____

Write and Draw to Express Yourself

Date: ___/___/___

Write and Draw to Express Yourself

Date: ___ / ___ / ___

Date: ___/___/___

Write and Draw to Express Yourself

Date: __/__/__
xmas

Write and Draw to Express Yourself

Date:

Write and Draw to Express Yourself

Date: ___ / ___ / ___

Write and Draw to Express Yourself

Date: ___ / ___ / ___

Christmas Time

Write and Draw to Express Yourself

Date: ___/___/___

Date: ___/___/___

Write and Draw to Express Yourself

Write and Draw to Express Yourself

Date: ___ / ___ / ___

Write and Draw to Express Yourself

Date:

Merry Christmas

Date: _______ / _____ / _______

Write and Draw to Express Yourself

Date: ___ / ___ / ___

Date: _______/____/______

Write and Draw to Express Yourself

Date: ___/___/___

Write and Draw to Express Yourself

Date: ___ / ___ / ___

Write and Draw to Express Yourself

Date: ___ / ___ / ___

Write and Draw to Express Yourself

Date: ___ / ___ / ___

Write and Draw to Express Yourself

Date: _____ / ___ / _____

Date: _____ / ___ / _____

Write and Draw to Express Yourself

Write and Draw to Express Yourself

Date: ___/___/___

Write and Draw to Express Yourself

The Magic of Christmas

Date: _____/_____/_____

Write and Draw to Express Yourself

Date: ___/___/___

Write and Draw to Express Yourself

Date:

Date: _____ / ____ / ______

Write and Draw to Express Yourself

Write and Draw to Express Yourself

Date: ___/___/___

Write and Draw to Express Yourself

Date: ___ / ___ / ___

Write and Draw to Express Yourself

Date: ___/___/___

Write and Draw to Express Yourself

Date: ___ / ___ / ___

Write and Draw to Express Yourself

Write and Draw to Express Yourself

peace
&
joy

Write and Draw to Express Yourself

Date:

Date: ____/____/____

Write and Draw to Express Yourself

Date: ___/___/___

Write and Draw to Express Yourself

Date:

Date: _______/____/____

Write and Draw to Express Yourself

Write and Draw to Express Yourself

Date: /   /

Write and Draw to Express Yourself

Date:

Date: ____/____/____

Write and Draw to Express Yourself

Date: ___/___/___

Date: ___/___/___

Write and Draw to Express Yourself

Date: